TRANSITIONS

ACKNOWLEDGMENTS

To Jack Stockman
of Oak Park, Illinois,
for the art work
on the cover.

To Erika Tiepel
of Littleton, Colorado,
for the layout
and design.

To Zondervan Bible Publishers
for permission to use the
Holy Bible: New International Version,

TRANSITIONS

SAVORING THE SEASONS OF LIFE

PETER MENCONI, RICHARD PEACE,
& LYMAN COLEMAN

DEVELOPED BY
SERENDIPITY
H O U S E

DISTRIBUTED BY
NAVPRESS ®
A MINISTRY OF THE NAVIGATORS

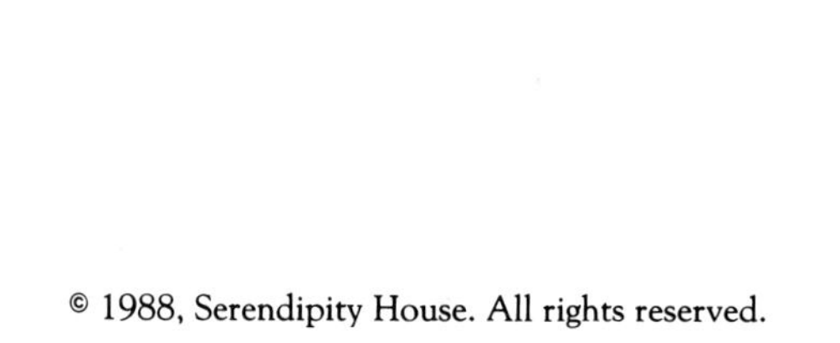

QUESTIONS ABOUT THIS COURSE FOR AN

ENTRY LEVEL SUPPORT GROUP

PURPOSE

1. **What is this course all about?** Becoming a support group while studying the Bible.

SEEKERS/ STRUGGLERS

2. **Who is it for?** Two kinds of people: (a) Seekers who do not know where they are with God but are open to finding out, and (b) Strugglers who are committed to Jesus Christ but need to grow in their faith.

ABY BOOMERS

3. **Who is this course specifically designed for?** While the course is for everyone, the series is primarily written for Baby Boomers.

NEW PEOPLE

4. **Does this mean that I can invite my "non-church" friends?** Absolutely, this is what this group is all about—giving people a chance to restart their spiritual pilgrimage.

STUDY

5. **What are we going to study?** Six causes of transitions (see inside front cover) and what the Bible has to say about each one.

AUTHORS

6. **Who wrote the material?** Peter Menconi (dentist/Consultant/free-lance writer), Richard Peace (seminary professor and free-lance consultant on media), and Lyman Coleman (group process trainer and writer).

DREAM

7. **What motivated them to write this course?** A dream to offer to Baby Boomers and others the chance to investigate the Christian life for a few weeks in a support group.

FIRST SESSION

8. **What do we do at the meetings?** In the first session, you get acquainted and decide on one of two Bible study tracks. In sessions two through seven, you follow the track you chose.

TWO TRACKS

9. **What are the two tracks?** Gospel Study or Epistle Study. The Gospel Study is a more basic, "entry-level" study with a questionnaire with multiple choice options. (None of the options are "right" or "wrong." They are designed to start you thinking.) The Epistle Study has open-ended questions that usually necessitate more involvement in the Scripture text.

CHOOSING

10. Which track of Bible Study do you recommend? The Gospel Study is best for newly-formed groups or groups that are unfamiliar with small group Bible study. The Epistle Study is best for deeper Bible study groups.

BOTH

11. Can you choose both? Yes, depending upon your time schedule.

Here's how to decide:

STUDY	APPROXIMATE COMPLETION TIME
Gospel Study only	40-60 minutes
Epistle Study only	40-60 minutes
Gospel and Epistle Study	80-120 minutes

HOMEWORK OPTION

12. What if we want to do both the Gospel and Epistle Studies but don't have time at the session? You can spend two weeks on a unit—the Gospel Study the first week and the Epistle Study the next. Or, you can do the Gospel Study in the session and the Epistle Study for homework.

BIBLE KNOWLEDGE

13. What if you don't know anything about the Bible? No problem. The Gospel Study is based on a parable or story that stands on its own—to discuss as though you are hearing it for the first time. The Epistle Study comes with complete Reference Notes—to keep you up to speed.

THE FEARLESS FOURSOME

HOW TO OVERCOME GROUP JITTERS!

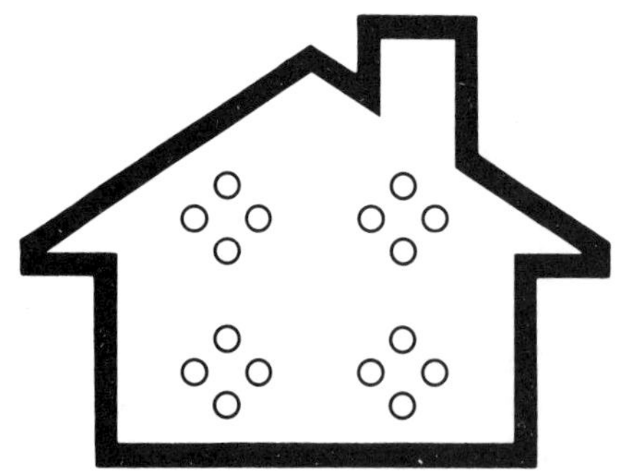

PROBLEM: A lot of people are afraid of groups.

SOLUTION: Divide into groups of 4 when the time comes for sharing. In 4's the quiet person will be able to talk, and the talkative person will not dominate as much. In fact, in 4's most of the problems of group dynamics will be avoided.

SO: When the time comes for sharing, ask 4 to sit around the dining table, 4 around the kitchen table, and 4 around a folding table in the family room.

REFERENCE NOTES

14. What is the purpose of the Reference Notes in the Epistle Study? To help you understand the context of the Bible passage and any difficult words that need to be defined.

LEADERSHIP

15. Who leads the meetings? One person can lead for the whole time—or you can rotate the leadership.

RULES

16. What are the ground rules for the group?

☐ Priority: While you are in the course, you give the group meetings priority.

☐ Participation: Everyone participates and no one dominates.

☐ Respect: Everyone is given the right to their own opinion and "dumb questions" are encouraged and respected.

☐ Confidentiality: Anything that is said in the meeting is never repeated outside the meeting.

☐ Empty Chair: The group stays open to new people at every meeting as long as they understand the ground rules.

☐ Support: Permission is given to call upon each other in time of need —even in the middle of the night.

CONTINUING

17. What happens to the group after finishing the course? The group is free to disband or continue to another course.
Call Toll Free 800-525-9563.

SESSION 1 Introduction

Some 2500 years ago, a Greek philosopher said, "There is nothing permanent except change." Change and transition are as inevitable as taxes and death. We cannot stop the onward march of our lives even if we wanted. But as we move through life, some of these changes can be anticipated. How we manage these transitions is important in our emotional and spiritual development.

In the following scriptural studies, we will look at some transitions and changes associated with adulthood. Specifically, we will examine the end of childhood, starting on our own, mid-life, and aging. In addition, we will examine the experiences of Baby Boomers and Empty Nesters. Through these group studies, we will see that the transitions of life offer opportunities for maturity and growth.

FYI

For Your Information

- The Baby Boomer generation is represented by the record 76 million people born between 1946 and 1964.
- By 1990, 57% of the adult U.S. population will have been born since World War II.
- While many people experience a "bumpy road" into mid-life, studies have shown that a "mid-life crisis" is not inevitable for everyone.
- The population of older people has grown from 18 million in 1965 to 28 million today.
- People older than 65 compose 12% of the population. This percentage is expected to rise to over 20% by the year 2030.

LEADER: IF YOU HAVE MORE THAN SEVEN PEOPLE AT THE MEETING SUBDIVIDE INTO GROUPS OF FOUR FOR SHARING (SEE BOX ON PAGE 6).

Orientation: In the first session, take some time to review the questions and answers on pages 5-7 about this course, especially the RULES for a support group under question 14.

STUDY

STEP ONE: The following questions will help introduce the topics of the remaining sessions. Answer the following questions and discuss your responses with your group.

1. When did you first become aware that your childhood had ended?
   - ___ before 10 years old
   - ___ around 10–12 years old
   - ___ around 13–15 years old
   - ___ around 16–18 years old
   - ___ after 18 years old

2. What circumstances or situations brought you to realize your childhood was over?

3. Why did you leave home to be on your own?
   - ___ I went to college
   - ___ I went into military service
   - ___ I got a job out of town
   - ___ I went to seek my fortune
   - ___ I was "kicked out"
   - ___ I got married
   - ___ I got an apartment of my own
   - ___ other ___________

4. If you were born between 1946 and 1964, you are one of the 76 million members of the Baby Boom generation. Which of the following statements best represents your perception of this group?
   - ___ This is the generation that wanted to be "forever young"
   - ___ This is the most scrutinized and analyzed generation ever
   - ___ Baby Boomers were expected to remake the world but haven't done it yet
   - ___ This generation has turned traditional values upside down
   - ___ Baby Boomers have avoided or postponed commitments to others
   - ___ Baby Boomers are the most educated and idealistic generation yet
   - ___ This generation believes that it "can have it all"
   - ___ This generation has brought positive changes to America
   - ___ Baby Boomers have difficulty with sacrifice and lowered expectations
   - ___ Baby Boomers are skeptical of big business and government
   - ___ Baby Boomers have developed a new version of materialism

5. How do/did you feel about becoming 40 years old?

____ It is/was no "big deal"

____ I do not look forward to it

____ I found it to be traumatic

____ I feel like it's a 100 years away

____ I felt like I was finally an adult

____ I felt like I was "over the hill'

____ I haven't thought about it

____ I can't wait to get there

____ I was depressed

____ I can't image being 40

____ I went into crisis

____ I made/will make the best of it

____ I dread it

6. Did you have a hard time leaving home and living on your own? Did you have a hard time when your children left home? Why? Why not? (Answer the applicable questions.)

7. Which one of the following statements best describes your attitude toward aging?

____ I accept it as a natural progression of life

____ I will fight it every way I can

____ I want to grow old "gracefully"

____ I look forward to every "season of life"

____ I am depressed by the thought of growing old

____ I plan to stay as active as possible as I age

____ I hope I never grow old

REFLECT

STEP TWO: As time allows, discuss with your group your agreement or disagreement with the following statements.

- It is the nature of a man as he grows older . . . to protest against change, particularly change for the better.

  — *John Steinbeck*

- Middle age is when you stop criticizing the older generation and start criticizing the younger one.

  — *Laurence J. Peter*

SESSION 2
End of Childhood

Usually, we are not aware of the end of childhood until later. But as we look back on our lives, we realize that an event or a series of events has marked the end of childhood. Generally in our culture, we move from childhood to adolescence. In many other cultures, the end of childhood is celebrated by a ceremonial rite of passage where a person moves directly from childhood to adulthood. (In America, the Jewish Bar Mitzvah and the Christian Confirmation are examples of such "rites of passage.")

In Luke 2:41–52 we see Jesus at the age of 12 going through his transition from childhood to adulthood. During this transition, we see a difference in perspective between Jesus and his parents. We also are aware that both Jesus and his parents "grow" through this experience. When childhood ends, relationships with others become more intentional. The spontaneous love of childhood gives way to the more deliberate love of adolescence and adulthood. The Apostle Paul recognized this in his much-quoted dissertation on love in 1 Corinthians 13. In the following studies, we will look at the challenges and opportunities that come with the passing of childhood.

OPTION 1

Gospel Study/Rite of Passage

OPEN

STEP ONE: Answer the following questions and share your responses with your group.

1. At age 12, where were you living? How many of you were gathered around the family table at that time? What were your family conversations like?

LEADER: IF YOU HAVE MORE THAN SEVEN PEOPLE AT THE MEETING, DIVIDE INTO GROUPS OF FOUR FOR SHARING (SEE BOX ON PAGE 6).

2. How would you rate your maturity at the age of 12?
   ____ I was too mature for my own good
   ____ I was quite immature
   ____ I thought I was more mature than I really was
   ____ I was about as mature as other 12-year-olds
   ____ I didn't know what was going on when I was 12
   ____ I considered myself almost to be an adult

3. Relative to other 12-year-olds, in what area (physical development, social skills, athletic performance, etc.) did you feel "more mature"? In what one area did you feel "less mature"?

STUDY

STEP TWO: Read Luke 2:41–52 and discuss your responses to the following questions with your group.

***41**Every year his parents went to Jerusalem for the Feast of the*
***Passover. 42**When he was twelve years old, they went up to the Feast,*
***according to the custom. 43**After the Feast was over, while his parents*
were returning home, the boy Jesus stayed behind in Jerusalem, but
***they were unaware of it. 44**Thinking he was in their company, they*
traveled on for a day. Then they began looking for him among their
***relatives and friends. 45**When they did not find him, they went back to*
***Jerusalem to look for him. 46**After three days they found him in the*
temple courts, sitting among the teachers, listening to them and
***asking them questions. 47**Everyone who heard him was amazed at his*
***understanding and his answers. 48**When his parents saw him, they*
were astonished. His mother said to him, "Son, why have you treated
us like this? Your father and I have been anxiously searching for you."
***49**"Why were you searching for me?" he asked. "Didn't you know I*
***had to be in my Father's house?" 50**But they did not understand what*
he was saying to them.
***51**Then he went down to Nazareth with them and was obedient to*
***them. But his mother treasured all these things in her heart. 52**And*
Jesus grew in wisdom and stature, and in favor with God and men.

Luke 2:41–52 NIV

1. What was your first significant time apart from your parents or "coming of age" experience as a teenager? (What was significant about it?)
 a. Summer camp in the mountains
 b. Confirmation class week or spiritual retreat
 c. Field trip to the "big city," sponsored by others
 d. Field trip to the "big city," on your own
 e. Getting a summer job with room and board elsewhere

2. What do you think is significant about Jesus being 12 years old in this passage?
 a. He would soon become a man
 b. His parents allowed him to roam Jerusalem without them
 c. He was old enough to discuss the law with the teachers in the Temple
 d. He had finished school and could now teach his elders
 e. He could now participate fully in the Passover Feast

3. Why did Jesus stay behind in Jerusalem after his parents had left?
 a. He didn't realize that they were gone
 b. He was more interested in "city lights"
 c. He needed to be about the work of his heavenly Father
 d. He wanted to learn as much as he could while in Jerusalem

4. Why do you think it took Jesus' parents so long to discover he was missing?
   a. They thought that he was playing with the other children in the caravan
   b. They usually let Jesus "shift for himself"
   c. They thought he was with friends and relatives
   d. They didn't particularly care what Jesus did because he was now a "man"

5. How do you think Mary and Joseph felt as they searched for Jesus?
   a. They were probably quite angry
   b. They were confident they would find him
   c. They were probably "worried sick"
   d. They were trusting God to make all come out well
   e. They were feeling quite guilty about leaving Jesus

6. Why did Jesus spend his time in the Temple courts?
   a. He was trying to hide from his parents
   b. He was trying to learn all he could from the teachers
   c. He was "showing off" his knowledge to the teachers
   d. He was trying to prepare himself for future ministry

7. Why were the teachers astonished by Jesus' understanding?
   a. Because 12-year-olds usually didn't know as much as Jesus did
   b. Because Jesus was more mature than most 12-year-olds
   c. Because Jesus' understanding exceeded theirs
   d. Because Jesus didn't have any formal schooling

8. Why was Jesus surprised that his parents were searching for him?
   a. Because Jesus went off on his own often
   b. Because Jesus' heavenly perspective clouded his earthly understanding of his parents
   c. Because Jesus assumed that they understood his motivation
   d. Because Jesus assumed that his parents thought like he did

9. How would you describe Jesus' relationship with his parents?
   a. He was a disobedient child
   b. He obeyed his earthly parents when they didn't conflict with his heavenly Father
   c. He was a model child
   d. He loved his parents but gave top priority to his heavenly Father
   e. He did whatever he wanted
   f. His mother knew that he was someone special and treated him accordingly

10. What do we learn about Jesus' development in these verses?
   a. Jesus developed healthy relationships with both God and man
   b. Jesus learned his lessons well
   c. Jesus gained respect because of what he knew and how he acted
   d. Jesus had little effect on other people
   e. Jesus was moving into manhood

REFLECT

STEP THREE: Answer the following questions and discuss your responses with your group.

1. When you realized that your childhood was over, how did you feel?

____ sad	____ introspective
____ bewildered	____ dreamy
____ eager	____ carefree
____ unaffected	____ raring to go
____ mixed up	____ sober

2. What things about your own childhood would you change?

3. How can you improve childhood experiences for your children or for children to whom you relate regularly?

OPTION 2

Epistle Study/Maturing Love

OPEN

STEP ONE: Start with the OPEN questions on page 11.

STUDY

STEP TWO: Read 1 Corinthians 13 and share your responses to the following questions with your group. If you do not understand a particular word or phrase, check the Reference Notes on page 16.

1And now I will show you the most excellent way. If I speak in the
tongues of men and of angels, but have not love, I am only a
resounding gong or a clanging cymbal. 2If I have the gift of prophecy
and can fathom all mysteries and all knowledge, and if I have a faith
that can move mountains, but have not love, I am nothing. 3If I give all
I possess to the poor and surrender my body to the flames, but have
not love, I gain nothing.
4Love is patient, love is kind. It does not envy, it does not boast, it
is not proud. 5It is not rude, it is not self-seeking, it is not easily
angered, it keeps no record of wrongs. 6Love does not delight in evil
but rejoices with the truth. 7It always protects, always trusts, always
hopes, always perseveres.

[8]Love never fails. But where there are prophecies, they will cease; where there are tongues, they will be stilled; where there is knowledge, it will pass away. [9]For we know in part and we prophesy in part, [10]but when perfection comes, the imperfect disappears. [11]When I was a child, I talked like a child, I thought like a child, I reasoned like a child. When I became a man, I put childish ways behind me. [12]Now we see but a poor reflection as in a mirror; then we shall see face to face. Now I know in part; then I shall know fully, even as I am fully known.

[13]And now these three remain: faith, hope and love. But the greatest of these is love.

1 Corinthians 13 NIV

1. What type of love is Paul writing about here? When have you experienced a love anything like this?

2. Why is love more important than eloquent speech, superior knowledge, and sacrifical giving?

3. What are the major characteristics and responsibilities of love outlined in verses 4-7? What is the opposite of this kind of love?

4. Why does Paul say that "love never fails"?

5. Why can our knowledge of reality be only partial?

6. Is love, as described in this chapter, more characteristic of children or mature adults? Why?

7. Why is love greater than faith and hope?

REFLECT

STEP THREE: As time allows, discuss with your group your agreement or disagreement with the following statements.

- Our only realistic hope as I see it is to bring up our children with a feeling that they are in this world not for their own satisfaction, but primarily to serve others.

  — Dr. Benjamin Spock

- There are only two lasting bequests we can hope to give our children. One of these is roots; the other wings.

  — Hodding Carter

APPLY

STEP FOUR: Answer the following questions and share your responses with the group.

1. Think of specific ways in which your relationships with others changed when you became an adult. For example, how did your relationship change with your parents? Your siblings? Your peers?

2. Which aspects of love have you mastered? In which areas do you still need to work?

REFERENCE NOTES

Summary . . . In this soaring hymn in praise of love (which has become a classic piece of literature) Paul first points out (vv. 1-3) the primacy of love (in contrast to other religious activities); then he describes love itself (vv. 4-7), and ends (vv. 8-13) by pointing out love's enduring quality (in contrast, once again, to other religious activities). As Karl Barth outlines the chapter: "It is love alone that counts (vv. 1-3); it is love alone that triumphs (vv. 4-7); it is love alone that endures (vv. 8-13)."

vv. 1-3 **. . .** If a person does not love, neither spiritual gifts, nor good deeds, nor martyrdom is of any ultimate value to that person. Love is the context within which these gifts and deeds become significant.

v. 1 **tongues of men and of angels . . .** Ecstatic speech—highly prized in Corinth—is an authentic gift of the Holy Spirit; however, it becomes like the unintelligible noise of pagan worship when used outside the context of love.

gong/cymbal . . . Paul is probably thinking of the repetitious and meaningless noise generated at pagan temples by beating on metal instruments.

v. 2 **. . .** Paul contrasts three other spiritual gifts with love: prophecy, knowledge, and faith.

prophecy . . . Such activity is highly commended by Paul (e.g., 14:1); yet without love even a prophet is really nothing.

fathom all mysteries . . . In Corinth, special, esoteric knowledge was highly prized (1:18-2:16), but even if one knew the very secrets of God, without love it would be to no end. That which makes a person significant (i.e., the opposite of *nothing*) is not a gift like prophecy or knowledge, but it is the ability to love.

faith that can move mountains . . . Paul refers to Jesus' words in Mark 11:23—even such massive faith that can unleash God's power in visible ways is not enough to make a person significant without love at its foundation.

v. 3 **give all I possess to the poor . . .** Presumably Paul refers to goods and property given to others but not in love. The point is not: do not give if you cannot do so in love (the poor still profit from the gifts regardless of the spirit in which they are given), but rather that the loveless giver gains no reward on the day of judgment.

surrender my body . . . Not even the act of the martyr—giving up one's very life for the sake of another or in a great cause—brings personal benefit when it is done outside love.

vv. 4-7 . . . By way of definition, Paul tells us what love does and does not do. He defines love in terms of action and attitude.

v. 4 **patient . . .** This word describes patience with people (not circumstances). It characterizes the person who is slow to anger (long suffering) despite provocation.

kind . . . In fact, the loving person does good to those who provoke him/her.

not envy . . . The loving person does not covet what others have nor begrudge them their possessions.

not boast . . . The loving person is self-effacing, not a braggart.

not proud . . . Literally, not "puffed up." The loving person does not feel others to be inferior nor does he/she look down on people.

v. 5 **not rude . . .** The same Greek word is used in 7:36 to describe a man who led a woman on but then refused to marry her.

not self-seeking . . . The loving person not only does not insist on his/her rights, but will give up his/her due for the sake of others.

not easily angered . . . The loving person is not easily angered by others; s/he is not touchy.

keeps no record of wrongs . . . The verb is an accounting term and the image is of a ledger sheet on which wrongs received are recorded. The loving person forgives and forgets.

v. 6 **does not delight in evil . . .** The loving person does not rejoice when others fail (which could make him/her feel superior) or enjoy pointing out wrong in others.

rejoices with the truth . . . Paul shifts back to the positive.

v. 7 **trusts . . .** Literally "believes all things" i.e., "never loses faith."

hopes . . . Love does not lose hope.

perseveres . . . Love keeps loving despite hardship.

vv. 8-12 **. . .** Having described love, Paul once again contrasts love with spiritual gifts, emphasizing this time the permanent quality of love over the transitory nature of the *charismata*.

v. 8 **Love never fails . . .** In the sense that it functions both now and in the age to come. The *charismata* are relevant only to this age.

cease/be stilled/pass away . . . One day, when God comes again in fullness, prophecy will be fulfilled (and so cease); the indirect communication with God via tongues will no longer be needed (so they are stilled); and since all will be revealed and evident, secret knowledge about God will be redundant (and so pass away). Each of these are partial revelations about God, vital in this present age but unnecessary in the age to come.

v. 11 **. . .** The contrast is between the age (when we are all still children) and the age to come (where we are fulfilled).

v. 12 **Now/then . . .** Paul is thinking of the Second Coming; the flowering of the New Age in fullness when God reveals himself, in contrast to the here and now—when, although the New Age has been initiated, it is still incomplete.

poor reflection . . . Corinth was famous for the mirrors it made out of highly polished metal. Still, no mirror manufactured in the first century was without imperfections. All of them distorted the image somewhat; and so this is an apt metaphor for the present knowledge of God. It is marred.

v. 13 **remain . . .** Charismatic gifts will cease because they brought only partial knowledge of God, but three things will carry over into the New Age: faith, hope, and love.

SESSION 3
On Your Own

Leaving the comfort and security of our parents' home for the first time can be both a heady and scary experience. There are many reasons why we finally make the break. Sometimes these reasons are voluntary and planned; other times, they are sudden and disorienting. In many ways the "on your own" experience is similar to the growing eaglet who gets his wings and is prodded from the nest. As the maturing eaglet leaves the aerie, he must decide where to go, what to eat, and how to survive.

In the Gospel Study of Matthew 4:1-17, we see Jesus on his own and fighting for survival. We can learn much from the way Jesus handled this experience. In the Epistle Study we see that as Christians we are never really "on our own." Christians are interdependent members of a universal "body" of believers with Christ as the "head."

You are not on your own with these studies. You have the other group members to interact with on these important and interesting scriptural passages.

OPTION 1

Gospel Study/ Preparing for Flight

OPEN

STEP ONE: Answer the following questions and share your responses with your group.

LEADER: IF YOU HAVE MORE THAN SEVEN PEOPLE AT THE MEETING, DIVIDE INTO GROUPS OF FOUR FOR SHARING (SEE BOX ON PAGE 6).

1. When you left home to be on your own, how did you feel? Why?

___ excited	___ determined	___ enthusiastic
___ scared	___ terrified	___ melancholy
___ ready	___ confident	___ happy
___ reluctant	___ jittery	___ optimistic

2. Where were you going at the time? What "piece of home" did you take with you? How long before you returned "home"?

STUDY

STEP TWO: Read Matthew 4:1-17 and discuss your responses to the following questions with your group.

1Then Jesus was led by the Spirit into the desert to be tempted by the devil. 2After fasting forty days and forty nights, he was hungry. 3The tempter came to him and said, "If you are the Son of God, tell these stones to become bread."

4Jesus answered, "It is written: 'Man does not live on bread alone, but on every word that comes from the mouth of God.' "

5Then the devil took him to the holy city and had him stand on the highest point of the temple. 6"If you are the Son of God," he said, "throw yourself down. For it is written:

" 'He will command his angels concerning you, and they will lift you up in their hands, so that you will not strike your foot against a stone.' "

7Jesus answered him, "It is also written; 'Do not put the Lord your God to the test.' "

8Again, the devil took him to a very high mountain and showed him all the kingdoms of the world and their splendor. 9"All this I will give you," he said, "if you will bow down and worship me."

10Jesus said to him, "Away from me, Satan! For it is written: 'Worship the Lord your God, and serve him only.' "

11Then the devil left him, and angels came and attended him.

12When Jesus heard that John had been put in prison, he returned to Galilee. 13Leaving Nazareth, he went and lived in Capernaum, which was by the lake in the area of Zebulun and Naphtali—14to fulfill what was said through the prophet Isaiah:

15"Land of Zebulun and land of Naphtali, the way to the sea, along the Jordan, Galilee of the Gentiles—16the people living in darkness have seen a great light; on those living in the land of the shadow of death a light has dawned."

17From that time on Jesus began to preach, "Repent, for the kingdom of heaven is near."

Matthew 4:1-17 NIV

1. What has been your experience of the "desert"—that time apart in some cultural or spiritual wasteland when you felt all aone, "in between," and without your familiar surroundings and dependable resources?

2. Why did the Spirit take Jesus into the desert?
   a. Jesus had to go through the "School of Hard Knocks"
   b. Jesus was young and idealistic and needed a lesson in reality
   c. Jesus wanted to put the devil in his place
   d. Jesus needed to be toughened for the difficult years of ministry ahead

3. Why did the devil tempt Jesus with turning the stones to bread?
   a. He was actually taunting and mocking Jesus
   b. He was attacking Jesus at his most vulnerable point
   c. He wanted to get Jesus to obey him one step at a time
   d. He was trying to control Jesus

4. What do we learn from Jesus' response to this first temptation?
   a. That spiritual "food" is more important than physical food
   b. That physical temptation can be overcome by focusing on God
   c. That physical temptation is easy to overcome
   d. That it is possible to overcome temptation even when weak and vulnerable

5. What is the nature of Satan's second temptation?
   a. He is questioning Jesus' authority as the Son of God
   b. He is again trying to get Jesus to obey him
   c. He is attacking Jesus' pride
   d. He is using Old Testament Scripture to tempt Jesus

6. What do we learn about the devil in the last temptation?
   a. That Satan is tenacious
   b. That Satan is "dense" and didn't get the message the first two times
   c. That Satan's motive all along was to get Jesus to worship him
   d. That he will try every "angle" to get us to yield

7. What is your reaction to Jesus' rebuff of Satan?
   a. Jesus treated the devil too rudely
   b. Jesus should have "nailed" him sooner
   c. Jesus finally lost his patience and his temper
   d. Jesus powerfully affirmed the need to worship God only

8. In what way(s) was Jesus now "on his own"?
   a. He now needed to preach repentance because John the Baptist was in prison
   b. He had survived his wilderness testing and was now ready to start his earthly ministry
   c. He had not yet called any of his 12 disciples and therefore was preaching alone
   d. He was away from home and the people he loved

REFLECT

STEP THREE: Answer the following questions and share your responses with your group.

1. What advice would you give to one who is starting out on his/her own?

2. If you could start your adult life over again, what would you change?

3. In what ways can you still live out your childhood dreams?

OPTION 2

Epistle Study/One for All

OPEN

STEP ONE: Start with the OPEN questions on page 20.

STUDY

STEP TWO: Read Ephesians 4:1-16 and answer the following questions and discuss your responses with your group. If you do not understand a particular word or phrase, check the Reference Notes on page 25.

***
[1]As a prisoner for the Lord, then, I urge you to live a life worthy of
the calling you have received. [2]Be completely humble and gentle; be
patient, bearing with one another in love. [3]Make every effort to keep
the unity of the Spirit through the bond of peace.[4]There is one body
and one Spirit—just as you were called to one hope when you were
called—[5]one Lord, one faith, one baptism; [6]one God and Father of all,
who is over all and through all and in all.
[7]But to each one of us grace has been given as Christ
apportioned it. [8]This is why it says:
"When he ascended on high, he led captives in his train and gave
gifts to men."
[9](What does "he ascended" mean except that he also descended
to the lower, earthly regions? [10]He who descended is the very one
who ascended higher than all the heavens, in order to fill the whole
universe.) [11]It was he who gave some to be apostles, some to be
prophets, some to be evangelists, and some to be pastors and
teachers, [12]to prepare God's people for works of service, so that the
body of Christ may be built up [13]until we all reach unity in the faith
and in the knowledge of the Son of God and become mature,
attaining to the whole measure of the fullness of Christ.
[14]Then we will no longer be infants, tossed back and forth by the
waves, and blown here and there by every wind of teaching and by the
cunning and craftiness of men in their deceitful scheming. [15]Instead,
speaking the truth in love, we will in all things grow up into him who
is the Head, that is, Christ. [16]From him the whole body, joined and
held together by every supporting ligament, grows and builds itself
up in love, as each part does its work.***

Ephesians 4:1-16 NIV

1. What do you associate with the experience of "calling"?
   a. Dinner-time: "Call me anything, but don't call me late for dinner"
   b. Name-calling: "Sticks and stones will break my bones, but names will never hurt me"
   c. Prospecting by phone: Cold calls to find one sale item, one date, or one baby sitter
   d. Volunteer duty: When someone calls you to take their place
   e. "Bad news": From IRS, police, doctor, pastor, lawyer

2. What "calling" does Paul have in mind here? To what are we called as Christians?

3. What is the source of Christian unity?

4. What does each Christian bring to the "body of Christ"?

5. Are spiritual gifts only for the spiritually mature? Why? Why not?

6. What part do spiritual gifts place in fostering Christian unity? In fostering Christian maturity?

7. What are the major differences between an "infant" Christian and a more mature Christian?

8. Why are we never really "on our own" as Christians?

REFLECT

STEP THREE: As time allows, discuss with your group your agreement or disagreement with the following statements.

- Man finds it hard to get what he wants, because he does not want the best; God finds it hard to give, because He would give the best, and man will not take it. — *George MacDonald*

- Many babes in Christ die in infancy because of their inability to live up to the impossible standards which are thrown upon them by more mature(?) believers, who so often fall short in those standards themselves. — *James Sennett in* The Wittenburg Door

APPLY

STEP FOUR: Answer the following questions and share your responses with your group.

1. If you had to compare your spiritual life to the stages of growth of a person, where would you be right now? In infancy? Early adolescence? Young adulthood? Mid-life crisis? Somewhere inbetween?

2. Do you tend to overestimate or underestimate your gifts?

3. If you were to compare your Bible study group to a symphony orchestra, what would it sound like?

4. What is one wish you would like to make for your group?

REFERENCE NOTES

Summary . . . Paul begins the second half of his epistle by calling for all Christians to lead "a life worthy" of the grand plan they have been called to be part of.

Paul begins chapter 4 by focusing on those attitudes, actions, and insights that foster *unity* within the body (vv. 1-6). Then he shifts his emphasis to the *diversity* of gifts and functions within the one body (vv. 7-13). He ends by pointing to the maturity produced by such diversity within unity (vv. 14-16).

v. 1 **a prisoner for the Lord . . .** In 3:1 Paul described himself as "the prisoner of Christ Jesus"—reflecting the fact that while legally he was the prisoner of Rome, spiritually he was the prisoner of Christ Jesus. Here in 4:1 he maintains the same dual insight—he is a prisoner but his true (and willing) bondage is not to Caesar but to Christ.

a life worthy . . . This is the theme of the remainder of Ephesians. Having described the creation by God of his new society, Paul now defines the lifestyle of this new race of people (Christians).

v. 2 **. . .** Paul identifies the five qualities of life that promote unity between people: humility, gentleness, patience, natural forbearance, and love.

humble . . . The very first attitude Paul urges for Christians is that of humility. It is interesting that within Greek culture, *humility* was not seen as a virtue. Humility was viewed as cringing subservience and was therefore despised. The Greeks defined humility as "the crouching submissiveness of a slave" (F.F. Bruce). Christians, however, came to understand humility in quite a different way. Humility was understood to be an absence of pride and self-assertion (both of which are sources of discord) based on accurate self-knowledge and on an understanding of the God-given worth of others. Humility is a key to the growth of healthy relationships between people.

gentle . . . The RSV translates this word as "meekness." But Paul is not urging people to be timid and without convictions. Gentleness "is not a synonym for 'weakness.' On the contrary, it is the gentleness of the strong, whose strength is under control. It is the quality of a strong personality who is nevertheless master of himself and the servant of others" (Stott).

be patient . . . Patience is "slowness in avenging wrong or retaliating when hurt by another" (Foulkes).

v. 3 **Make every effort . . .** What Paul is saying is this: "Work zealously at maintaining in visible form what has already been achieved for you by Christ and is therefore a fact."

unity . . . This is what each of the virtues in verse 2 aims at: the close bonding of people to one another. While verse 4 indicates that what is in view is the unity of the Christian church, these same attitudes build unity in all kinds of relationships: within marriage, across generations, between groups.

the bond of peace . . . This peace has been made possible through Jesus Christ who first reconciled humanity to God (bringing peace with God) and then reconciled people to one another (creating a bond of peace between them).

vv. 4-6 **. . .** The unity Paul is urging is based on the three-fold work of the triune God. God the Holy Spirit creates the one body (v. 3). God the Son brings hope, faith, and baptism to this body (vv. 4-5); while God the Father fills the body (v. 6).

v. 4 **one . . .** It is very hard to miss Paul's stress on unity. He repeats the word *one* some seven times in three verses. In fact, given the rhythm and phrasing of verses 4-6, it seems likely that Paul is quoting an ancient Christian hymn, or a catechism.

one body and one Spirit . . . It is the indwelling Holy Spirit that maintains this single body—the church—within which Jew and Gentile come together.

vv. 4-5 **hope/faith/baptism . . .** Jesus Christ is the object of the Christian hope and faith. He is the One in whose name they are baptized (Gal. 3:27).

v. 5 **one Lord . . .** Since all Christians are indwelt by the same person and filled with the same power, there is a deep and natural affinity of one Christian for another. The title *Lord* means "Master." The "Lord" is the one from whom direction is received and obeyed.

vv. 7-13 **. . .** From a discussion of unity (vv. 1-6) Paul turns here to a discussion of diversity. As he will show, unity does not mean uniformity.

v. 8 **. . .** Paul quotes Psalm 68:18 in which is described the triumphal procession of a conquering Jewish king up Mt. Zion and into Jerusalem. The king is followed by a procession of prisoners in chains. As he marches up the hill, he is given gifts of tribute and in turn disperses gifts of booty. Paul uses this verse to describe Christ's ascension into heaven. The captives that follow along behind him are the principalities and powers that he has defeated (see 1:20-22; Col. 2:15). The gifts that the conquering Christ disperses are gifts of ministry given to his followers.

v. 9 **descended . . .** Paul is referring to Christ's incarnation whereby he came down from heaven and invaded space and time (see Phil. 2:5-11). He may also be referring to Christ's death and subsequent invasion of hell (see 1 Pet. 3:19, 4:6).

v. 11 **. . .** This is one of several lists of gifts (see 1 Cor. 12:8-10, 28-30; Rom. 12:6-8). No single list is exhaustive, defining all the gifts. Each is illustrative. The emphasis in this list is on teaching gifts.

apostles . . . Paul probably had in mind the small group of men who had seen the resurrected Christ and been commissioned by him to launch his church (see Acts 1:21-22; 1 Cor. 9:1). In this sense there are no longer any apostles, yet "it is certainly possible to argue that there are people with apostolic ministries of a different kind, including episcopal jurisdiction, pioneer missionary work, church planting, itinerant leadership, etc." (Stott).

prophets . . . In contrast to teachers who relied on the Old Testament Scripture and the teaching of Jesus to instruct others, prophets offered words of instruction, exhortation, and admonition that were immediate and unpremeditated. Their source was direct revelation from God.

evangelists . . . In the early centuries of the church, these were the men and women who moved from place to place, telling the gospel story to those who had not heard it and/or believed it. While all Christians are called on to be witnesses of the gospel, the reference here is to those with the special gift of evangelism. The gift of evangelism is the ability to make the gospel clear and convincing to other people.

pastors and teachers . . . The way in which this is expressed in Greek indicates that these two functions reside in one person. In a day when books were rare and expensive, it was the task of the pastor/teacher not only to look after the welfare of the flock (the title *pastor* means, literally, "shepherd") but to preserve the Christian tradition and instruct people in it.

v. 12 **prepare . . .** These teaching gifts are to be used to train *everyone* in the church so that *each* Christian is capable of ministry. In other words, the prime task of the clergy is to train the laity to do ministry. This stands in contrast to many churches where the laity hire clergy to do ministry. In 3:12 Paul taught the concept of the "priesthood of all believers." Here he teaches "the ministry of all believers."

vv. 13-16 **. . .** The aim of all these gifts is to produce *maturity*. Maturity is, in turn, vital to unity—the theme with which Paul began this section.

v. 15 **speaking the truth in love . . .** Christians are to stand for both truth and love. Both are necessary. Truth without love becomes harsh. Love without truth becomes weak.

SESSION 4
Baby Boomers

If you were born between 1946 and 1964, you are one of 76 million "card-carrying" members of the Baby Boom generation. The post-World War II years saw a rapid, dramatic increase in the birth rate, which continued until the mid-1960s. The 1950s and '60s saw crowded elementary school classrooms. The late 1960s and '70s saw this overcrowding strain secondary schools and colleges.

The Baby Boom generation has other unique characteristics. This was the first generation to grow up with TV and rock music. In his book *Great Expectations,* Landon Jones notes that the Baby Boomers were the first generation to be isolated and targeted for mass marketing. (In 1955, Disney's "Davy Crockett" series produced a 9-month boom in coonskin caps.) The media and advertisers are still targeting this generation as they enter middle age.

The Baby Boom generation has also had its traumas. They have seen their heroes die violently—John Kennedy, Martin Luther King, Bobby Kennedy. They opposed the Vietnam War and resisted the draft. Baby Boomers have experienced campus unrest and seen our cities burn. This generation with its "great expectations" has had to deal with some jarring realities.

In the 1970s, many Baby Boomers turned from trying to change the world to trying to change themselves. Their emphasis on "self-actualization" gave rise to the label "the Me-Generation." In the '80s, this quest was theologized into the New Age Movement. Today, ministry to this generation offers both an opportunity and a challenge.

LEADER: IF YOU HAVE MORE THAN SEVEN PEOPLE AT THE MEETING, DIVIDE INTO GROUPS OF FOUR FOR SHARING (SEE BOX ON PAGE 6).

In Matthew 19:16-30, the rich young man reflects many of the characteristics of today's Baby Boomer. We can learn much from the way Jesus interacts with him. In 1 Timothy 6:3-10, we see that none of us is free from the temptation to "love money." In their lifetime many Baby Boomers have known nothing but affluence. And this generation seems particularly attracted to it. The Epistle Study will allow us to interact with a Biblical perspective of money.

OPTION 1

Gospel Study/ Lifestyles of the Rich and Famous

OPEN

STEP ONE: How much of a Baby Boomer are you? Take the following "Baby Boomer Trivia Quiz" and discuss your responses with your group.

1. A Dove Bar is:
   a. a bar of soap
   b. a lapel pen wore by charismatics
   c. a gourmet ice cream bar
   d. a famous singles' lounge

2. Crosby, Stills, and Nash is/are:
   a. a prestigious law firm
   b. a '70s pop/rock group
   c. three cars no longer being manufactured
   d. a crooner, opera singer, and humorist

3. Fettucine Alfredo is:
   a. an Italian opera star
   b. a Chicago "hit man"
   c. a pasta dish
   d. the current President of Italy

4. Maddie and David are:
   a. two guys who sell mail-order fruit
   b. private eyes with the Blue Moon Detective Agency
   c. first 2 people to walk on the moon
   d. Wall Street's most successful "inside traders"

5. "The Big Chill" is:
   a. a king-size cola at 7-11
   b. the very cold winter of '83
   c. East-West politics
   d. a movie about '60s nostalgia

6. Based on this self-scoring quiz and other better-known characteristics of Baby Boomers, how well do you fit in with this generation? Are you "in" or "out"? How far in, or how far out?

STUDY

STEP TWO: Read Matthew 19:16-30 and discuss your responses to the following questions with your group.

16Now a man came up to Jesus and asked, "Teacher, what good thing must I do to get eternal life?"

17"Why do you ask me about what is good?" Jesus replied. "There is only One who is good. If you want to enter life, obey the commandments."

18"Which ones?" the man inquired.

Jesus replied, "Do not murder, do not commit adultery, do not steal, do not give false testimony, 19honor your father and mother,' and 'love your neighbor as yourself.' "

20"All these I have kept," the young man said. "What do I still lack?"

21Jesus answered, "If you want to be perfect, go, sell your possessions and give to the poor, and you will have treasure in heaven. Then come, follow me."

22When the young man heard this, he went away sad, because he had great wealth.

23Then Jesus said to his disciples, "I tell you the truth, it is hard
for a rich man to enter the kingdom of heaven. 24Again I tell you, it is
easier for a camel to go through the eye of a needle than for a rich man to enter the kingdom of God."

25When the disciples heard this, they were greatly astonished and asked, "Who then can be saved?"

26Jesus looked at them and said, "With man this is impossible, but with God all things are possible."

27Peter answered him, "We have left everything to follow you! What then will there be for us?"

28Jesus said to them, "I tell you the truth, at the renewal of all things, when the Son of Man sits on his glorious throne, you who have followed me will also sit on twelve thrones, judging the twelve
tribes of Israel. 29And everyone who has left houses or brothers or
sisters or father or mother or children or fields for my sake will
receive a hundred times as much and will inherit eternal life. 30But
many who are first will be last, and many who are last will be first."

Matthew 19:16-30 NIV

1. In what ways are you like the rich young man?
   a. We are both smug, even a bit self-righteous
   b. We are searching for truth, each in our own way
   c. We both believe we can "have it all"
   d. We are both captive to our wealth
   e. We are as different as night and day
   f. He has riches and youth, I have ______________________________

2. What do you think motivated the young rich man to ask Jesus his question?
   a. He was sincerely searching to know spiritual truth
   b. He was feeling self-righteous and wanted affirmation from Jesus
   c. He had almost everything, but needed an "eternal life insurance policy"
   d. He was testing Jesus' knowledge as a teacher

3. Why did Jesus answer his question with another question?
   a. Jesus thought it was a stupid question
   b. Jesus thought the man should have known the answer to his question
   c. Jesus understood the young man's insincere motives
   d. Jesus was trying to get the young man to think for himself

4. Why did Jesus use the word *life* instead of "eternal life"?
   a. Because he saw eternal life as an extension of earthly life
   b. Because he was trying to confuse the rich young man
   c. Because obedience to God and the commandments was to be actualized on earth
   d. Because a new birth into eternal life happens during our earthly life

5. What do you think of Jesus' reply?
   a. It was to be expected
   b. It was totally unreasonable
   c. It makes me wonder about my own relationship with Jesus
   d. It underscored the importance of placing Christ first

6. What was Jesus saying about rich people?
   a. He didn't like them
   b. Their money often becomes their god
   c. They can't buy their way into heaven
   d. Preoccupation with wealth often distracts them from serving God

7. Why do you think Peter responded the way he did in verse 27?
   a. He was jealous of the rich young man
   b. He felt that his commitment to Jesus had cost him financially and materially
   c. He wanted to know how he would be rewarded
   d. He felt like he was shut out of "the action"

8. What is Jesus trying to teach us in this passage?
   a. That commitment to him must be total
   b. That wealth and relationships are unimportant
   c. That service to God is priority #1
   d. That, in due time, service to him will be rewarded
   e. That eternal life is more important than earthly life

APPLY

STEP THREE: Baby Boomers have often been criticized for being "too materialistic." Perhaps this can be said about most Americans. Answer the following questions and discuss your responses with your group.

1. Do you think most people in the U.S. are "too materialistic"? Explain.

2. If you could cut back on your financial commitments or get rid of some of your "material" obligations, would you do it? Why or why not?

3. Where could you start simplifying your life?

OPTION 2

Epistle Study/Having It All

OPEN

STEP ONE: Start with the OPEN questions on page 30.

STUDY

STEP TWO: Read 1 Timothy 6:3-10 and discuss your responses to the following questions with your group. If you do not understand a particular word or phrase, check the Reference Notes on the next page.

3If anyone teaches false doctrines and does not agree to the sound instruction of our Lord Jesus Christ and to godly teaching, 4he is conceited and understands nothing. He has an unhealthy interest in controversies and quarrels about words that result in envy, strife, malicious talk, evil suspicions 5and constant friction between men of corrupt mind, who have been robbed of the truth and who think that godliness is a means to financial gain.

[6]But godliness with contentment is great gain. [7]For we brought nothing into the world, and we can take nothing out of it. [8]But if we have food and clothing, we will be content with that. [9]People who want to get rich fall into temptation and a trap and into many foolish and harmful desires that plunge men into ruin and destruction. [10]For the love of money is a root of all kinds of evil. Some people, eager for money, have wandered from the faith and pierced themselves with many griefs.

1 Timothy 6:3-10 NIV

1. What is your experience with "false doctrine"? Is it something you come across every day at work, every week in church, only on campus, or only in the cultic fringes of society? Cite a recent example.

2. What are some contemporary examples of people using Christianity as a means to financial gain?

3. How does "godliness with contentment" contrast with "having it all"?

4. A prevalent philosophy of our day is that "the one with the most toys wins." How does this philosophy contrast with verses 7 and 8?

5. What are some potential pitfalls when pursuing wealth?

6. Is money and materialism a unifying force or a divisive force in relationships between people? Explain your response.

7. Why is "the love of money" the root of all kinds of evil?

REFLECT

STEP THREE: As time allows, discuss with your group your agreement or disagreement with the following statements.

- If a rich man is proud of his wealth, he should not be praised until it is known how he employs it.

  — *Socrates*

- Money is a terrible master but an excellent servant.

  — *P.T. Barnum*

APPLY

STEP FOUR: Answer the following questions and share your responses with the group.

1. What is the special temptation for you when it comes to money?

2. If you could reduce your financial commitments and simplify your lifestyle, would you do it? Why or why not? Where would you cut back if you decided to do so?

REFERENCE

Summary . . . In this passage Paul summarizes the problem of false teachers and Timothy's role in dealing with them. In the process he provides some more details about the false teachers. It turns out that what motivates them is pride, a love of argument, and greed (vv. 3-5). However, what really ought to motivate us, Paul says, is "godliness with contentment" (vv. 6-10).

vv. 3-5 **. . .** False doctrine, Paul says, brings negative results. Those who have departed from the teaching of Jesus are people of dubious character who have brought disharmony into the church.

v. 3 **the sound instruction of our Lord Jesus Christ . . .** This is their error. They have departed from the teaching of Jesus.

v. 4 **he is conceited and understands nothing . . .** This is the first thing Paul says about these teachers. They are swollen with pride when, in fact, they are really quite ignorant. The NEB puts it well: they are "pompous ignoramus[es]"!

unhealthy interest . . . This is literally "being sick or diseased."

controversies . . . This is more than just "disputes." The word refers to a sort of idle speculation. They were preoccupied "with pseudo-intellectual theorizings" (Kelly).

quarrels . . . This is literally a "battle of words," which Paul sharply criticizes. He "paints in lurid colours the pride from which it springs, the spirit of anti-social bitterness and suspicion which it sows in the church, and the moral degeneracy which it eventually produces. The picture is a savage one, and although some of the details may be borrowed from conventional catalogues of vices, it suggests a concrete situation which excited Paul's distress and indignation" (Kelly).

result in . . . Paul identifies two negative results of this sick preoccupation with word battles. First, if produces strife within the church, and second, it brings about a kind of corruption or decay to the minds of the teachers themselves.

envy . . . Controversy produces jealousy as people pick sides.

v. 5 **corrupt mind . . .** *Mind* refers not just to "the power of reason" but to one's whole way of thinking.

robbed of the truth . . . Such corruption results in the loss of the very truth of the gospel.

godliness is a means to financial gain . . . As Paul has hinted in 3:3 and 8, the bottom line motivation of these false teachers is the money they make from their teaching. Paul does not consider it wrong for a person to be paid for teaching (see 5:17-18), but he is incensed when greed is the main motivation for ministry.

vv. 6-10 **. . .** Paul picks up on this problem of greed and says two things about it. First, godliness is to be much preferred to profit (vv. 6-8), and second, a love of money brings dire results.

v. 6 **. . .** "This verse stands in immediate contrast to the last words in verse 5, with a striking play on terms. *They* think godliness 'is a way to become rich.' *Well* (Gk., *de,* "indeed"), they are right. There *is* great profit (now used metaphorically) in godliness *(religion does make a person very rich),* provided it is accompanied by a 'contented spirit' (Moffatt, Kelly), that is, *if* one *is satisfied with what* one *has* and does not seek material gain" (Fee).

contentment . . . This was a favorite word of the Stoic philosophers from whom Paul borrowed it. (Zeno, the founder of this philosophical school came from Tarsus, Paul's hometown.) This word refers to a person who is not impacted by circumstances. Such a person is self-contained and thus able to rise above all conditions. For Paul, however, this sort of contentment was derived from the Lord (see Phil. 4:11).

vv. 7-8 **. . .** There are two reasons why "godliness with contentment" brings great gain. First, at death people can take nothing with them, so why worry about material gain that has to be given up in the end anyway? Second, if people have the essentials in life, this should be enough.

vv. 9-10 **. . .** Paul ends by pointing out the dangers of riches. In these verses he chronicles the downward process that begins with the desire "to get rich." Such a desire leads into "temptation," which is, in turn, "a trap." The "trap" is the "many foolish and harmful desires" that afflict the greedy person. The end result is that such people are "plunge[d] . . . into ruin and destruction."

v. 9 **temptation . . .** Greed causes people to notice and desire what they might not otherwise have paid attention to.

v. 10 **For the love of money is a root of all kinds of evil . . .** Paul is probably quoting a well-known proverb in order to support the assertion he makes in verse 9 that the desire for money leads to ruin. This verse is often misquoted as "money is the root of all evil". While Paul clearly sees the danger of money, he is not contending that *all* evil can be traced to avarice.

some people . . . have wandered . . . Here is the problem. Some of the false teachers have given in to the temptation to riches. They were probably once good leaders in the church but they got caught by Satan (4:1-2), became enamored with speculative ideas (6:3-5), and in the end were pulled down by their love for money.

SESSION 5
Mid-Life

There is one gift we receive on our 40th birthday that most of us would rather not accept—middle age. There is a common notion that, after 40, life picks up speed as we go "over the hill." But while mid-life does have some limitations, it also can be a time of reevaluation, redirection, and recommitment. For most of us, mid-life is a period of transition and not crisis.

During the mid-life transition, many of us are knocked off balance. The "fast-starter," who was cruising through early adulthood, suddenly feels like "the wheels are coming off." Now many of his (her) early choices and actions are creating problems. Perhaps his marriage is sputtering or his relationships with his children are deteriorating. By contrast, the "slow-starter," who had been spinning his wheels through early adulthood, gets traction and takes off. Slowly but steadily, he begins to see many of his earlier choices come to fruition. Either scenario brings transition and change.

Also in mid-life, we must confront some realities that were easy to ignore during early adulthood. Mid-life resurrects many of the questions of adolescence and early adulthood, but in a more serious and urgent fashion. What is life all about? Who am I really? What am I doing with my life? How am I going to live the rest of my life? How can I make my life "count"? These and many other questions confront us as we realize our own mortality.

LEADER: IF YOU HAVE MORE THAN SEVEN PEOPLE AT THE MEETING, DIVIDE INTO GROUPS OF FOUR FOR SHARING (SEE BOX ON PAGE 6).

In John 3 we see Nicodemus wrestling with some of these mid-life questions. Jesus' response to Nicodemus will help us get a perspective on our own concerns. In the Epistle Study (Phil. 3:12-4:1), Paul takes a "mid-course" reading and looks to the remainder of life. Both studies give us insights into the mid-life transition.

OPTION 1

Gospel Study/ What's It All About . . . ?

OPEN

STEP ONE: Answer true or false to the following statements and discuss your responses with your group.

1. Mark each statement in this "mid-life quiz" true (T) or false (F). You'll find the answers at the back of the Gospel Study. After 40 . . .

- ____ most of us undergo some horrible mid-life crisis from which we never recover
- ____ exercising isn't worth the effort
- ____ your memory goes
- ____ losing the battle of the bulge is inevitable
- ____ it is harder to roll out of bed in the morning
- ____ your sex life crashes

2. The chart below shows thirteen possible stages of conversion in the spiritual journey of a person. Where are you now in your own spiritual journey?

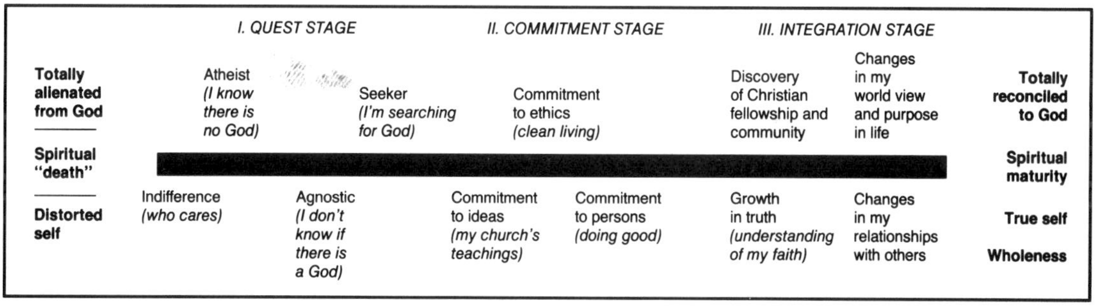

	I. QUEST STAGE					*II. COMMITMENT STAGE*		*III. INTEGRATION STAGE*		
Totally alienated from God		Atheist *(I know there is no God)*		Seeker *(I'm searching for God)*		Commitment to ethics *(clean living)*		Discovery of Christian fellowship and community	Changes in my world view and purpose in life	**Totally reconciled to God**
Spiritual "death"										**Spiritual maturity**
Distorted self	Indifference *(who cares)*		Agnostic *(I don't know if there is a God)*		Commitment to ideas *(my church's teachings)*		Commitment to persons *(doing good)*	Growth in truth *(understanding of my faith)*	Changes in my relationships with others	**True self** **Wholeness**

STUDY

STEP TWO: Read John 3:1–21 and discuss your responses to the following questions with your group.

[1]Now there was a man of the Pharisees named Nicodemus, a member of the Jewish ruling council. [2]He came to Jesus at night and said, "Rabbi, we know you are a teacher who has come from God. For no one could perform the miraculous signs you are doing if God were not with him."

[3]In reply Jesus declared, "I tell you the truth, no one can see the kingdom of God unless he is born again."

[4]"How can a man be born when he is old?" Nicodemus asked. "Surely he cannot enter a second time into his mother's womb to be born!"

***[5]Jesus answered, "I tell you the truth, no one can enter the
kingdom of God unless he is born of water and the Spirit. [6]Flesh gives
birth to flesh, but the Spirit gives birth to spirit. [7]You should not be
surprised at my saying, 'You must be born again.' [8]The wind blows
wherever it pleases. You hear its sound, but you cannot tell where it
comes from or where it is going. So it is with everyone born of the
Spirit."***

[9]"How can this be?" Nicodemus asked.

***[10]"You are Israel's teacher," said Jesus, "and do you not
understand these things? [11]I tell you the truth, we speak of what we
know, and we testify to what we have seen, but still you people do not
accept our testimony. [12]I have spoken to you of earthly things and you
do not believe; how then will you believe if I speak of heavenly things?
[13]No one has ever gone into heaven except the one who came from
heaven—the Son of Man. [14]Just as Moses lifted up the snake in the
desert, so the Son of Man must be lifted up, [15]that everyone who
believes in him may have eternal life.***

***[16]"For God so loved the world that he gave his one and only Son,
that whoever believes in him shall not perish but have eternal life.
[17]For God did not send his Son into the world to condemn the world,
but to save the world through him. [18]Whoever believes in him is not
condemned, but whoever does not believe stands condemned already
because he has not believed in the name of God's one and only Son.
[19]This is the verdict: Light has come into the world, but men loved
darkness instead of light because their deeds were evil. [20]Everyone
who does evil hates the light, and will not come into the light for fear
that his deeds will be exposed. [21]But whoever lives by the truth
comes into the light, so that it may be seen plainly that what he has
done has been done through God."***

John 3:1-21 NIV

1. At what points can you identify with Nicodemus in verses 1-2?
   a. Like me, he is an influential "VIP"
   b. Like me, he is an education person
   c. Like me, he is a religious person
   d. Like me, he is a hypocrite
   e. Like me, he is shy, not wanting to be identified with Jesus
   f. Like me, he is curious, always searching for truth
   g. Like me, he is a believer in Jesus

2. Why did Nicodemus come to Jesus at night?
   a. He was too busy during the day
   b. He didn't want others to see him
   c. He didn't find Jesus until evening
   d. He couldn't sleep and decided to talk to Jesus

3. What did Jesus mean when he said that it was necessary to be "born again"?
   a. That life starts anew at mid-life
   b. That we must be born anew by the Spirit
   c. That belief and faith in him would bring spiritual rebirth and eternal life
   d. That we would have to wait until we died to experience spiritual rebirth

4. Why was Nicodemus confused?
   a. Because he thought only in earthly terms
   b. Because he didn't want to understand
   c. Because Jesus was talking spiritual "mumbo jumbo"
   d. Because spiritual truths are not always easy to understand
   e. Because Jesus was purposely trying to confuse him

5. What is/are the major question(s) that Nicodemus is actually asking Jesus?
   a. Who are you really?
   b. How do you perform those miracles?
   c. How can I have eternal life?
   d. What is life all about?
   e. Who am I and what am I doing here?

6. What is/are the major teaching(s) in this Scripture?
   a. Jesus is the only way to eternal life
   b. Forgiveness of sin comes only through Jesus
   c. God's plan to save the world was finalized with Jesus' birth and earthly life
   d. Faith in Jesus brings forgiveness of sin and eternal life
   e. God loves the world

7. What is Jesus saying about "light and darkness"?
   a. Light makes right/down with darkness
   b. We are all in darkness/he is light
   c. Darkness hides our sin and evil/light exposes them
   d. God gives light and truth/evil gives darkness and falsehood

8. Two of the major questions of mid-life are "who am I?" and "what am I doing with my life?" How does Jesus answer these questions in this passage?
   a. He doesn't answer them
   b. He implies that we are created by God in order to love and serve him
   c. He states that eternal life follows this earthly life
   d. He states that we are created by God to love others
   e. He states that we are created by God to straighten out an evil world

APPLY

STEP THREE: Answer the following questions and discuss your responses with the group.

Which of the following "unavoidable concerns" (cited by Jim Conway) are you most concerned about as you face "life after 40"?

a. Learning to love again when I was so hurt the first time
b. Developing a sexy marriage with my one and only
c. Finding a job that I can love
d. Aging with finesse
e. Assisting children with transition
f. Parenting my own parents
g. Preparing for a recreative retirement
h. Preparing for death to come "sooner or later"
i. Making my life count for something, now and for eternity

OPTION 2

Epistle Study/ Mid-Course Correction

OPEN

STEP ONE: Start with the OPEN questions on page 39.

STUDY

STEP TWO: Read Philippians 3:12-4:1 and discuss your responses to the following questions with your group. If you do not understand a particular word or phrase, check the Reference Notes on page 44.

[12]Not that I have already obtained all this, or have already been
made perfect, but I press on to take hold of that for which Christ
Jesus took hold of me. [13]Brothers, I do not consider myself yet to
have taken hold of it. But one thing I do: Forgetting what is behind
and straining toward what is ahead, [14]I press on toward the goal to
win the prize for which God has called me heavenward in Christ
Jesus.
[15]All of us who are mature should take such a view of things. And
if on some point you think differently, that too God will make clear to
you. [16]Only let us live up to what we have already attained.
[17]Join with others in following my example, brothers, and take
note of those who live according to the pattern we gave you. [18]For, as
I have often told you before and now say again even with tears, many
live as enemies of the cross of Christ. [19]Their destiny is destruction,
their god is their stomach, and their glory is in their shame. Their
mind is on earthly things. [20]But our citizenship is in heaven. And we
eagerly await a Savior from there, the Lord Jesus Christ, [21]who, by the
power that enables him to bring everything under his control, will
transform our lowly bodies so that they will be like his glorious body.
[1]Therefore, my brothers, you whom I love and long for, my joy and
crown, that is how you should stand firm in the Lord, dear friends!

Philippians 3:12-4:1 NIV

1. As for your image of what "mid-life" entails, do you envision/experience it as being more like a *pioneer* (never content, always pushing on to new things), or as a *settler* (content to stay put once you've arrived and to grow wherre you are)? Give an example.

2. How does Paul assess his level of spiritual maturity?

3. Of what is Paul trying to "take hold"?

4. How does Paul relate to the past? To the future?

5. What is "the prize" toward which he is moving?

6. What is the mature perspective Paul is advocating?

7. What are some characteristics of other lifestyles that are contrary to a mature Christian lifestyle?

8. What might be Paul's response to the criticism that "Christians are so heavenly-minded that they are no earthly good"?

9. For Christians at mid-life, what should be their perspective on life?

REFLECT

STEP THREE: As time allows, discuss with your group your agreement or disagreement with the following statements.

- Middle age is the time when a man/woman is always thinking that in a week or two s/he will feel as good as ever.

  — *Don Marquis*

- The long, dull, monotonous years of middle-aged prosperity or middle-aged adversity are excellent campaigning weather for the Devil.

  — *C.S. Lewis*

APPLY

STEP FOUR: Answer the following questions and share your responses with the group.

1. What has been the main issue in your spiritual pilgrimage up to the mid-point of your life (or where you now are if you are under 40)?

2. How has the issue or issues changed in the second half of life? (Or if you have yet to reach 40, what do you imagine you will have to deal with in the second half of your pilgrimage?)

REFERENCE NOTES

Summary . . . In the next passage Paul will lay bare his heart to the Philippians. He'll describe how in contrast to his former reliance on an impeccable heritage and on zealous striving to obey the law, now his driving passion was that of "knowing Christ." This is what motivated him. This is what consumed him. In this passage he describes in more detail what it means to "strive to take hold of Christ." Here he also warns against anyone who might feel that they have already "arrived" spiritually and thus attained "perfection." Over against this pattern of striving to know Christ (vv. 12-14), which he enjoins the Philippians to follow (vv. 15-17), Paul sets the pattern modeled by the false teachers (vv. 18-19).Their concern is with food laws and circumcision—"earthly things"—in contrast to the heavenly Kingdom to which Christians belong.

v. 12 **Not that . . .** Paul disclaims having reached any sort of perfection in his spiritual life or in fully comprehending who Christ is.

obtained . . . This probably refers to comprehending fully on a mental and spiritual level just who Jesus Christ is.

all this . . . In Greek it is not clear what Paul is referring to by this phrase. Is he looking backward at what he just said about attaining the resurrection (vv. 10-11)? Is he looking forward to what he will say about the prize at the end of the race (v. 14)? The best guess is that his reference is to Christ himself. Thus what Paul is asserting is that he has not yet fully comprehended intellectually, emotionally, or spiritually the magnificence of Jesus Christ. This is why he must continue to "press on" and "strain" forward in his spiritual pilgrimage.

perfect . . . This is the only time in his epistles that Paul uses this word. He might be borrowing it from the vocabulary of the mystery religions. They offered to devotees the "secret" that would enable them to attain a sort of blissful perfection that would end their earthly struggles. In contrast Paul indicates that he has not yet fully understood Jesus Christ. There is simply too much to know of Christ ever to grasp it all this side of heaven. Thus the Jewish teachers are wrong when they say that if people are circumcised and keep the law, they can attain perfection.

press on . . . In contrast to those groups that claim it is possible to attain spiritual perfection here and now, the Christian life is one of relentless *striving* to know Christ in his fullness. The word Paul uses here describes a hunter who is diligently pursuing his quarry.

to take hold of . . . This is a difficult word to translate. It can refer to winning a prize, as for example, in a race. Or it can mean to understand or comprehend something.

Jesus took hold of me . . . Paul refers here to his conversion experience on the Damascus road.

v. 13 **consider . . .** This word means "to calculate precisely." Paul means that after looking carefully at his life and all he has experienced of Christ, he has come to the conclusion that he has a long way to go in his spiritual pilgrimage.

Forgetting what is behind . . . In order to press on to a successful conclusion of his spiritual pilgrimage, Paul must first cease looking at his past. He must forget past failures (such as persecuting the church). He must also forget past successes (such as reaching the pinnacle of Jewish spirituality). Neither guilt nor personal attainment will assist him in gaining Christ.

straining . . . In Paul's mind is the image of a race in a stadium with a runner straining every muscle as he propels himself around the track, not looking over his shoulder, conscious only of the finish line ahead. Christians are like runners in mid-race between the starting point (when Jesus laid hold of them) and the goal with its promised prize (which will be given at the resurrection).

what is ahead . . . If the first movement in the spiritual pilgrimage is to forget the past, the second movement is to concentrate fully on what lies ahead—full comprehension of Jesus Christ. Christians are lured forward by what the future holds instead of simply running away from their destructive past.

v. 14 **goal . . .** This is the mark on the track that signifies the end of the race.

the prize . . . In keeping with his stadium metaphor, what Paul seems to have in mind is the moment at the end of the race when the winner is called forward by the games master to receive the victory palm or wreath. Likewise, on the day of resurrection the Christian will be called forward by God to receive the prize, which is full knowledge of Christ Jesus.

v. 15 **mature . . .** This is the same word that is translated "perfect" in verse 12. He uses this word in a slightly ironic way here: Those of us who might think we are 'perfect' know that there is no such thing as true perfection. There is only continual striving to comprehend Christ.

v. 17 **following my example . . .** Paul does not mean to imply that he has somehow attainted the perfection they seek. On the contrary, he has already disclaimed such. What he is calling them to imitate is his striving to find his goodness in Christ Jesus, his willingness to give himself sacrifically for the sake of others, and his deep passion to see the gospel advance (1:12-26; 3:7-11).

the pattern . . . Paul has defined the pattern for the Christian life as forgetting what is behind and constantly forging ahead to grasp on all levels of one's being the fullness of Jesus Christ.

vv. 18-19 **. . .** In contrast to the Christian lifestyle is the pattern followed by the Jewish evangelists. In describing these men, once again Paul resorts to harsh and furious language.

v. 18 **enemies of the cross . . .** It was the fact of Jesus' death that so scandalized the Jews. They found it almost impossible to accept that God could will and work through a crucified Messiah.

v. 19 **destruction . . .** Since they reject the cross, which lies at the heart of the way of salvation, their destiny is to live outside the life offered by God in Christ. "Thus, because these Jews reject out of hand the only one who can save them, preserve their souls, and give them life, there is nothing left but for them to experience the opposite—loss, destruction, death—the utter ruin of their lives" (Hawthorne).

their god is their stomach . . . The Jews were obsessed with laws relating to what they could eat and drink, how and when to eat, ritual preparation for eating, etc. A key feature of their religious life thus involved the issue of food.

shame . . . By this word Paul is probably referring to nakedness and thus this is a reference to circumcision, which was another key feature of the Jewish religious life. In other words, food laws and circumcision had become gods to these people (Hawthorne).

v. 20 **citizenship . . .** In contrast to the Jewish teachers whose focus is on "earthly things" (v. 19), the focus of Christians is on heaven where their true home lies. This is a particularly apt image for the Philippians who lived as citizens of Rome and yet were in fact a long distance from the mother city itself. So too Christians live as citizens of heaven even though they have yet to attain it.

v. 21 **our lowly bodies . . .** In contrast to those who taught that perfection was possible here and now, Christians knew that it was only at the Second Coming, by the work of Christ, that their frail, weak, and corrupt bodies would be transformed into a spiritual body akin to Christ's "glorious body."

SESSION 6
Empty Nester

Another transition that is noteworthy takes place when your children leave home to strike out on their own. This so-called "empty-nest" time is dreaded by some and anticipated by others. The empty-nest transition period sees the end of one way of life and the beginning of another. Now the food bills lessen; there is less wash to do; there are no more tuition payments; the house is strangely quiet.

While there are few examples in the Bible that represent the empty-nest transition, several passages help to emphasize important characteristics of this period of life. In the account of Jesus raising the widow's son, we confront the feelings associated with loss. Needless to say, the issue of loss is often a major concern during the empty-nest transition. In Philippians 3:1-11, Paul also teaches us about loss—"loss for the sake of Christ."

OPTION 1

Gospel Study/In the Loss Column

OPEN

STEP ONE: Answer the following questions and share your responses with your group.

1. If you had to give up one modern convenience in your life, what would you give up? (First and last)

____ telephone	____ car
____ indoor toilet	____ stereo
____ electric lights	____ books
____ television	____ workshop
____ dishwasher	____ micro-wave

LEADER: IF YOU HAVE MORE THAN SEVEN PEOPLE AT THE MEETING, DIVIDE INTO GROUPS OF FOUR FOR SHARING (SEE BOX ON PAGE 6).

2. What is the most significant loss you have experienced in your life? That is, loss of . . .

____ a best friend	____ hope
____ a job	____ health
____ a loved one	____ your savings
____ your self-respect	____ a close relationship
____ your youth	____ other ____________

STUDY

STEP TWO: Read Luke 7:11-17 and discuss your responses to the following questions with your group.

***11**Soon afterward, Jesus went to a town called Nain, and his*
*disciples and a large crowd went along with him. **12**As he approached*
the town gate, a dead person was being carried out—the only son of
his mother, and she was a widow. And a large crowd from the town
*was with her. **13**When the Lord saw her, his heart went out to her and*
he said, "Don't cry."
***14**Then he went up and touched the coffin, and those carrying it*
*stood still. He said, "Young man, I say to you, get up!" **15**The dead man*
sat up and began to talk, and Jesus gave him back to his mother.
***16**They were all filled with awe and praised God. "A great prophet*
has appeared among us," they said. "God has come to help his
*people." **17**This news about Jesus spread throughout Judea and the*
surrounding country.

Luke 7:11-17 NIV

1. Which character in the story do you most readily identify with and why?
   a. The widow, because I have experienced the end of a relationship
   b. The mother, because my kids mean so much to me
   c. The dead person, because I once was lost, but now am found
   d. The young man, because I am just beginning to walk spiritually
   e. The crowd, because I am continually awed by Jesus and want to publish his good news as broadly as I can
   f. The Lord, because I don't like to see anyone cry or suffer alone

2. Why was it important that Jesus' disciples and a large crowd be with him?
   a. To verify what was about to happen
   b. To give him moral support
   c. To learn more about him from the miracle
   d. To allow him to "perform" for them
   e. To learn more about love and compassion

3. How do you imagine the mother felt?
   a. Her pain was unimaginable
   b. She was grateful for all the support of friends
   c. She liked all the attention
   d. She felt helpless and alone

4. What do we learn about Jesus in this story?
   a. Jesus understands our pain
   b. Jesus really doesn't know what it means to be human
   c. Jesus is always ready to show compassion
   d. Jesus cares what happens to individual people

5. How would you have reacted if you were in the crowd?
   a. I wouldn't have believed my eyes
   b. I'd believe that the young man had not really been dead
   c. I'd bow down and worship Jesus
   d. I'd be "scared stiff"

6. What do you think motivated Jesus to perform this miracle?
   a. He wanted to demonstrate his power over death
   b. He had immediate compassion for the woman
   c. He wanted to relieve the mother's suffering
   d. He wanted to impress the disciples and crowd with his deity

7. In what ways would the woman have been an "empty-nester"?
   a. She would no longer have close friends
   b. She would no longer have any children at home
   c. She would have lost both her husband and her son
   d. She knew what it was like to experience major loss

APPLY

STEP THREE: Answer the following questions and share your responses with your group.

1. Depending on your situation, answer one of the following questions:
   - What was it like for your parents when you and your siblings all left home?
   - What was it like (or will it be like) for you when your children left (or leave) home?
   - What was it like for a couple you know when their children left home?

2. What "advice" might you give to those facing an empty nest?

OPTION 2

Epistle Study/ Changes for the Better

OPEN

STEP ONE: Start with the OPEN questions on page 48.

STUDY

STEP TWO: Read Philippians 3:1-11 and answer the following questions and discuss your responses with your group. If you do not understand a particular word or phrase, check the Reference Notes on page 52.

1Finally, my brothers, rejoice in the Lord! It is no trouble for me to write the same things to you again, and it is a safeguard for you.

2Watch out for those dogs, those men who do evil, those mutilators of the flesh. 3For it is we who are the circumcision, we who worship by the Spirit of God, who glory in Christ Jesus, and who put no confidence in the flesh — 4though I myself have reasons for such confidence.

If anyone else thinks he has reasons to put confidence in the flesh, I have more: [5]circumcised on the eighth day, of the people of Israel, of the tribe of Benjamin, a Hebrew of Hebrews; in regard to the law, a Pharisee; [6]as for zeal, persecuting the church; as for legalistic righteousness, faultless.

[7]But whatever was to my profit I now consider loss for the sake of Christ. [8]What is more, I consider everything a loss compared to the surpassing greatness of knowing Christ Jesus my Lord, for whose sake I have lost all things. I consider them rubbish, that I may gain Christ [9]and be found in him, not having a righteousness of my own that comes from the law, but that which is through faith in Christ—the righteousness that come from God and is by faith. [10]I want to know Christ and the power of his resurrection and the fellowship of sharing in his sufferings, becoming like him in his death, [11]and so, somehow, to attain to the resurrection from the dead.

Philippians 3:1-11 NIV

1. If you had to brag about one thing you can do better than anyone else, what would it be? (If you have trouble with this one, you can pull out your "brag book" of family pictures and brag about one of your children.)

2. No matter what life's circumstances, why are we instructed to "rejoice in the Lord"?

3. According to verses 2-4, what is the major conflict of life that hinders us from rejoicing in the Lord?

4. What are some of the major changes and losses Paul experienced when he began to follow Christ?

5. How does Paul view these changes and losses?

6. What changes and losses did you experience when you became a Christian?

7. How are we to view these changes and losses?

8. What does it mean to "know Christ"?

REFLECT

STEP THREE: As time allows, discuss with your group your agreement or disagreement with the following statements.

- When you're through changing, you're through. — *Bruce Barton*

- The only sense that is common in the long run, is the sense of change—and we all instinctively avoid it. — *E.B. White*

APPLY

STEP FOUR: Answer the following questions and share your responses with the group.

1. What is there in your life that you could "lose" and yet be the richer for it?

2. What is it that you need to "gain" in order to have a better foundation for living?

REFERENCE NOTES

Summary . . . In this passage Paul turns his attention to the false teachers who are troubling the church at Philippi. First, he describes them by means of three rather vivid terms (dogs, evil doers, mutilators), each of which punctures in some way their image of themselves (v. 2). Then, he points out the error in their teaching. They are saying that it is by keeping the law that one gains God's favor (v. 3). Next, to demonstrate that righteousness is not attained in this way, Paul describes his own background (vv. 4-6). He was the most orthodox of Jews, and yet when he met Jesus on the Damascus road, he came to realize that all his accomplishments and all the privileges afforded him because of his heritage were mere rubbish in comparison to knowing Christ (vv. 7-11).

v. 1 **safeguard . . .** Joy is a safeguard against those negative attitudes that bring disunity. A person who is rejoicing cannot simultaneously be grumbling or promoting his or her own interests, etc.

v. 2 **. . .** By means of strong and even abusive language, Paul warns the Philippians about the false teachers who oppose them.

dogs . . . This is a derogatory term used by Jews in the first century to describe Gentiles, given its force by the fact that Jews despised dogs. (They considered them "unclean.") But here Paul flings this curse back at the false teachers. They are, in fact, the real "dogs" because of the way in which they are perverting the truth of God.

men who do evil . . . The Jews considered themselves to be the only people who did good in the eyes of God. But once again Paul turns their self image upside down and contends that, in fact, *they* are really the evil-doers because they rely for their righteousness on their own good works instead of on God's grace. Thus, their good deeds actually turn out to be evil.

mutilators of the flesh . . . In Greek this is a pun that is difficult to translate. Instead of using the normal word for circumcision *(peritome),* here Paul uses a different word *(katatome)* that refers to the mutilation of the flesh, something that is forbidden by the Old Testament (see Lev. 21:5). Paul is saying that their circumcision is really mutilation. Not only is it of no value but it acutally goes against God's will.

v. 3 **circumcision . . .** This is the act of cutting away the foreskin of the male genital. It was originally a sign of the special relationship that had been established between God and the nation of Israel (see Gen. 17:9-14). However, Israel lost sight of the spiritual significance of this act and instead concentrated on the ritual aspect. In doing this, Israel forfeited its claim to a special relationship with God. The Christians had now become the *true* circumcision.

we who worship by the Spirit of God . . . This is the first of three phrases in verse 3 by which Paul demonstrates that Christians have become the true circumcision. Judaism had become a religion of external ritual, whereas Christian worship was not so much governed by law as it was by the inner prompting of the Spirit.

who glory in Christ Jesus . . . Jews prided themselves in the law and their observance of it, while Christians "boast of" (the literal meaning of "glory") Jesus who has brought them righteousness.

who put no confidence in the flesh . . . Here the word *flesh* probably means "unredeemed human nature." Christians do not rely upon personal striving as the basis for their rightousness.

vv. 4-11 **. . .** Paul anticipates the response of those Jewish enemies to what he has just said about the lack of value of law and ritual. He knows they will claim that he says all this because he is a Christian and not an authentic Jew. To answer this charge Paul lays out before them his rather substantial credentials as a Jew (vv. 4-6) and then he points out that all his accomplishments lack any ultimate value when it comes to obtaining the favor of God (vv. 7-11). This section parallels 2:6-11. Just as Jesus gave up his privilege and status in order to do God's will, so too did Paul, following the lead of his Lord.

v. 5 **eighth day . . .** It was on the eighth day after birth that a Jewish child (as opposed to a proselyte) was circumcised. Paul was a true Jew right from the time of his birth.

the tribe of Benjamin . . . The members of the tribe of Benjamin constituted almost an elite within Israel.

a Pharisee . . . Paul now moves from lineage to accomplishments. He first notes that he was a member of a small, very strict sect of especially devoted Jews who had dedicated their lives to the faithful observance of the whole law. In other words, he was one of the spiritual elite in Israel.

v. 6 **as for zeal, persecuting the church . . .** Zeal was a highly prized virtue among the Jews. It was regarded as one of the greatest qualities in the religious life.

faultless . . . To the best of his ability Paul tried to observe the whole law. Taken together, all the attributes of which he speaks in verses 5-6 mean that Paul was in every way the match of his opponents in Philippi. He had lived at the very pinnacle of Judaism.

v. 7 **But . . .** When looked at from one point of view, Paul would appear to have been a highly-privileged, highly-accomplished religious leader. But when looked at from another point of view, this so-called advantage is seen to be mere illusion. Paul now proceeds to evaluate his pedigree not from a Jewish point of view but from the point of view of his Christian faith.

profit/loss . . . Paul describes his change in outlook in terms of a balance sheet such as was used in business. What was once on the "profit" side of the ledger when he was a Pharisee has been shifted over to the "loss" side now that he is a Christian.

v. 8 **compared to . . .** Paul states why his former advantages had become a "loss." He discovered that only one thing had any ultimate value—knowing Christ Jesus— and knowing Christ did not come as a result of personal accomplishment.

rubbish . . . This is really quite a vulgar term, and refers to either "waste food bound for the garbage pit" or "human dung."

vv. 8-10 **. . .** Paul now identifies the three reasons why he counts his former privileges as mere "dung." They were useless in his desire (1) to "gain Christ," (2) to "be found in him" and so possess a righteousness that comes not from personal attainment but from faith in Christ, and (3) to "know Christ and the power of his resurrection."

v. 10 **the power of his resurrection . . .** Paul wants to experience personally the resurrected Christ in all his power (Eph. 1:18-21).

the fellowship of sharing in his sufferings . . . Not only does Paul want to experience inwardly the resurrected (and hence living) Christ, he also wants to experience the Jesus who died for his sins.

becoming like him . . . Paul coins a new word by which he expresses "the staggering idea that he and all believers are caught up into Christ and are indissolubly linked together with him to share with him in all the events of his life, including his death and resurrection" (Hawthorne). See also Romans 6:3-10 where this same concept is expressed.

v. 11 **. . .** Although believers experience in the here and now the power of the resurrection, there also awaits them a future resurrection when they will be free from sin and its ravages.

somehow, to attain . . . It is not that Paul doubts that he will be part of those who are raised to new life in Christ on the Last Day. Rather, in humility, he expresses his sense that it is solely by God's grace that he would gain such a gift.

SESSION 7
Aging

American society is getting older. Since 1965 the population of older people has grown from 18 million to 28 million today. While people over 65 currently comprise about 12% of the population, they will be over 20% of the population by the year 2030.

Yes, Americans are living longer and they are also living better. The financial, physical, and mental health of older people has improved significantly in just a few decades. Today, due to government spending, older Americans constitute a wealthier segment of our population. Medical advances and preventive medicine have greatly improved the health of older citizens. In fact, the average American, retiring at 63, has between 15 and 20 years of good health ahead. A recent Gallup survey found that Americans 65 and older are just as likely as those under 65 to exercise regularly. In addition, older Americans generally feel good about themselves. One recent survey found that 31% of those 60 and older said that the retirement years were the best years yet. That was more than those who opted for childhood, the teens, the 20s, 30s, 40s, or 50s.

In the following studies, we will look at two scriptural passages that relate to aging. In the Gosepl Study, we will see Jesus' last response to his aging mother. In the Epistle Study, we will look at the early church's response to the elderly in their community.

OPTION 1

Gospel Study/Age-Old Problem

OPEN

STEP ONE: Answer true or false to the following statements in the "Aging Quiz" and share your responses with your group.

LEADER: IF YOU HAVE MORE THAN SEVEN PEOPLE AT THE MEETING, DIVIDE INTO GROUPS OF FOUR FOR SHARING **(SEE BOX ON PAGE 6).**

AGING QUIZ

____ **1.** Most elderly people are socially isolated and alone
____ **2.** All 5 senses tend to decline in old age
____ **3.** One-tenth of the aged live in long-stay facilities like nursing homes
____ **4.** A person's height tends to decline in old age
____ **5.** Older people have more short-term illnesses than people under 65
____ **6.** Aged people have fewer accidents per driver than drivers under 65
____ **7.** Most elderly people live alone
____ **8.** Most elderly people work or would like to have some kind of work (including housework or volunteer work)

Answers are found at the end of the Gospel Study.

STUDY

STEP TWO: Read John 19:25-27 and discuss your responses to the following questions with your group.

25Near the cross of Jesus stood his mother, his mother's sister,
Mary the wife of Clopas, and Mary Magdalene. 26When Jesus saw his
mother there, and the disciple whom he loved standing nearby, he
said to his mother, "Dear woman, here is your son," 27and to the
disciple, "Here is your mother." From that time on, this disciple took
her into his home.

John 19:25-27 NIV

1. Which character in the story do you most readily identify with and why?
   a. Jesus' mother, because I have outlived my son and/or will be dependent on others
   b. Jesus' mother, because my son has seen to it that I am (will be) provided for in my old age
   c. The beloved disciple, because I have a close friendship with Jesus
   d. The beloved disciple, because I have been given responsibility for an aging parent
   e. The onlookers, because aging is not yet my concern

2. What do we learn about Jesus' mother?
   a. She followed her son everywhere
   b. She loved her son deeply
   c. She had a good "support system"
   d. She wanted to be with her son to the very end
   e. Her family was important to her

3. What feelings do you think Jesus had when he saw his mother?
   a. He felt helpless
   b. He felt compassion for her and the other women
   c. He was confident that his mother would be cared for
   d. He was in too much agony to be concerned about her
   e. He loved her and was still looking out for her welfare

4. What feelings do you think Mary was having as she watched her son die?
   a. She was confused
   b. She felt deep pain
   c. She realized that his death was necessary; therefore she was at peace
   d. She was angry with the injustice
   e. She felt like her life was over

5. John is described elsewhere as "the disciple whom Jesus loved." What responsibility was Jesus giving to John?
   a. To continue Jesus' earthly ministry
   b. To lead the disciples
   c. To take care of his mother
   d. To be responsible for all the women

6. Why did Jesus address his mother as he did?
   a. He was expressing his love for her
   b. It was the only thing he could say
   c. He was conveying his confidence in John
   d. He was dispensing his responsibility for her
   e. He was helpless and showed it

7. How do you feel about Jesus' actions?
   a. I probably would have done the same thing
   b. I think he should have planned ahead
   c. I think he did the right thing
   d. I think he was imposing on John

APPLY

STEP THREE: Answer the following questions and share your responses with your group.

1. In your opinion which of the following groups should take primary responsibility for the care of dependent elderly people?

   ____ the government ____ their families ____ churches

2. Why do you feel this way?

3. Have you had to take care of one or both of your elderly parents? How did you handle the responsibility?

4. In what practical ways can your church integrate elderly people into the whole of church life?

(Answers to "Aging Quiz"—Odds are false; evens are true)

OPTION 2

Epistle Study/Senior Partners

OPEN

STEP ONE: Start with the OPEN questions on page 56.

STUDY

STEP TWO: Read 1 Timothy 5:1-21 and share your responses to the following questions with your group. If you do not understand a particular word or phrase, check the Reference Notes on page 61.

1 Do not rebuke an older man harshly, but exhort him as if he were
your father. Treat younger men as brothers, 2 older women as
mothers, and younger women as sisters, with absolute purity.

3 Give proper recognition to those widows who are really in need.
4 But if a widow has children or grandchildren, these should learn first
of all to put their religion into practice by caring for their own family
and so repaying their parents and grandparents, for this is pleasing to
God. 5 The widow who is really in need and left all alone puts her hope
in God and continues night and day to pray and to ask God for help.
6 But the widow who lives for pleasure is dead even while she lives.
7 Give the people these instructions, too, so that no one may be open
to blame. 8 If anyone does not provide for his relatives, and especially
for his immediate family, he has denied the faith and is worse than an
unbeliever.

9 No widow may be put on the list of widows unless she is over
sixty, has been faithful to her husband, 10 and is well known for her
good deeds, such as bringing up children, showing hospitality,
washing the feet of the saints, helping those in trouble and devoting
herself to all kinds of good deeds.

11 As for younger widows, do not put them on such a list. For when
their sensual desires overcome their dedication to Christ, they want
to marry. 12 Thus they bring judgment on themselves, because they
have broken their first pledge. 13 Besides, they get into the habit of
being idle and going about from house to house. And not only do they
become idlers, but also gossips and busybodies, saying things they
ought not to. 14 So I counsel younger widows to marry, to have
children, to manage their homes and to give the enemy no
opportunity for slander. 15 Some have in fact already turned away to
follow Satan.

16 If any woman who is a believer has widows in her family, she
should help them and not let the church be burdened with them, so
that the church can help those widows who are really in need.

17 The elders who direct the affairs of the church well are worthy
of double honor, especially those whose work is preaching and
teaching. 18 For the Scripture says, "Do not muzzle the ox while it is
treading out the grain," and "The worker deserves his wages." 19 Do
not entertain an accusation against an elder unless it is brought by
two or three witnesses. 20 Those who sin are to be rebuked publicly, so
that the others may take warning.

[21]I charge you, in the sight of God and Christ Jesus and the elect angels, to keep these instructions without partiality, and to do nothing out of favoritism.

1 Timothy 5:1-21 NIV

1. When you were growing up, what proverb best describes how your family regarded the use of money in relation to future needs?
   a. "Waste not, want not"
   b. "Eat, drink, and be merry, for tomorrow you die"
   c. "You can't take it with you"
   d. "A penny saved is a penny earned"
   e. "Penny wise, dollar foolish"
   f. "You only go around once, so grab for all the gusto you can"
   g. "It is more blessed to give than to receive"

2. According to verses 1 and 2, how are older people to be treated?

3. How are the needs of widows to be met?

4. According to these verses, what are our responsibilities to our immediate family? To other relatives?

5. What do you think of the qualification requirements in verses 9-15?

6. What are the responsibilites of the local church in caring for widows?

7. What are some of the unique gifts and abilities that the elderly bring to the local church?

8. In the local church, do you think the elderly should be segregated from, integrated into, or assimilated with the rest of the congregation? Why?

REFLECT

STEP THREE: As time allows, discuss with your group your agreement or disagreement with the following statements.

- To grow old is to pass from passion to compassion.

  — *Albert Camus*

- When your friends begin to flatter you on how young you look, it's a sure sign you're getting old.

  — *Mark Twain*

- Growing old isn't so bad when you consider the alternative.

  — *Maurice Chevalier*

APPLY

STEP FOUR: Answer the following questions and share your responses with the group.

1. How would you like to spend your retirement years?

2. What key lessons have you learned about transitions in life from this series of Bible studies?

3. What topic would you like to tackle next as a group?

REFERENCE NOTES

Summary . . . In this section Paul continues his instructions to Timothy. He makes comments on Timothy's relationship to older and younger men and women (vv. 1-2), on the question of widows (vv. 3-16), and on the issue of elders (vv. 17-25).

v. 1 **rebuke/exhort . . .** Timothy will have to confront older men over the issue of false teaching. Paul tells him how to do it. It is not by means of harsh "rebuke" (the Greek word used here is related to the one used in 3:3 and translated "violent" or "one who strikes"). Instead, he is to "appeal" to them. He is to "urge" them. This is the same word translated "urge" in 1:3 and 2:1. In other words, in "exhorting" Timothy here in this letter, Paul is modeling for him how to interact with older men.

vv. 3-16 **. . .** Paul next deals with the first of two problem groups—younger widows. (The other problem group is the elders, which he will get to in verses 17-22.) He puts his instructions in the context of the larger issue: care of widows by the church. His concern is that Timothy distinguish between "widows who are really in need" (for whom the church must provide care) and those younger widows who really ought to remarry. The problem that has developed is with some of the younger widows who have become a divisive force in the church, perhaps because they have aligned themselves with the erring elders (see vv. 11-15; 2 Tim. 3:6-7). Paul uses "widows in need" as the positive example against which the activities of these younger widows are to be compared (in much the same way that he contrasts the erring elders to Timothy who is the model of what the Christian should be).

v. 3 **widows . . .** The early church, following the pattern of the Jewish nation before them, was committed to caring for those women who had lost their husbands.

v. 4 **. . .** The first group of widows who do not qualify for help are those who have family and friends who can care for them (vv. 8, 16). Greek law stated that children were legally bound to support their parents. Paul's reason is that care of parents is one way to carry out one's religious duties. In this way children will be "repaying" the parent or grandparent for care given them when young. Paul points out that this pleases God.

vv. 5-6 **. . .** Paul next contrasts two types of widow: those who have put their hope in God (v. 5) and those who by their sensual living give no evidence of trusting God to meet their needs (v. 6). The first group of widows are really "all alone" and so must trust God. The second group "live for pleasure." In the first century it was very difficult for a single woman to support herself. There were few jobs open to her so that some were driven to prostitution. It may be that Paul is contrasting those women who refuse to be compromised and so put their trust in God with those women who live by sensual means (whether in actual prostitution or by being involved with a particular man).

vv. 9-10 **. . .** Paul identifies three basic qualifications in order for the genuine widow to be supported by the church. He illustrates the last qualification ("good deeds") by means of four examples.

v. 9 **list of widows . . .** Some have argued (on the basis of second century and later documents) that Paul was here establishing an "order of widows" that served the church by their prayer (v. 5) and by their good deeds (i.e., via the duties listed in verse 10) in exchange for support. In fact, neither this text nor the later historical evidence supports this idea. Paul's real concern is with the younger widows and how their actions differ from these "widows in need" who deserve help.

sixty . . . In the first century, 60 was considered the age of retirement and the point at which "old age" began. It was also considered to be the age beyond which remarriage was not a real possibility.

v. 10 **bringing up children . . .** The first example of "good deeds" has to do with raising children, one's own and possibly also orphans.

showing hospitality . . . Inviting strangers into one's home is the second illustration of a "good deed."

vv. 11-15 **. . .** Paul now comes to the real issue, the problematic younger widows. He given two reasons for not putting them on the list for support. First, because their sexual desires are such that they do not want to remain widows (vv. 11-12), and second, because they are not really living in accord with the model of the godly widow that he has just sketched (v. 13). His advice is that they remarry (v. 14) lest they fall away from the faith (v. 15).

vv. 17-22 **. . .** Paul next turns to the second problematic group: the elders. As he did with widows, he treats the problem of elders in its larger context; in this case, the role and rights of all elders. Paul begins by stating his genuine concern that elders be honored and treated fairly (vv. 17-19). Then he deals with the tough problem of those elders who are, in fact, sinning (vv. 20-21) and ends with how to replace dismissed elders (v. 22) especially in light of the fact that the sins of some are not always obvious (v. 24).

vv. 17-18 **. . .** Paul says three things about elders. First, their role is to manage the affairs of the church. Second, this includes preaching and teaching. Third, they deserve to be paid for this service.

v. 17 **elders . . .** It is probably the term used for all leaders in the church, which would include overseers and deacons. These leaders were often literally "elder," i.e., older individuals.

vv. 19-20 **. . .** Paul next addresses the matter of discipline. He says two things. First, no unsubstantiated charge is to be made about an elder, and second, if valid charges are laid, those found guilty are to be rebuked publicly.

v. 19 **. . .** This was the normal pattern followed in the church when there was a dispute (see Deut. 19:15; John 8:17; 2 Cor. 13:1; Heb. 10:28). Such a public hearing would serve to protect a leader from frivolous or malicious charges.

v. 20 **the others . . .** A public rebuke will serve to warn other elders who are in error as well as the whole church.

v. 21 **. . .** It is important that this rule be applied across the board, even to those elders who might have great influence within the community.

Suggested Reading

From a Christian perspective:

Mid-Life: Psychological and Spiritual Perspectives, Janice Brewi and Anne Brennan, New York: Crossroads, 1982.

Stages of Faith, James Fowler, San Francisco: Harper and Row, 1981.

Mid-Life: A Time to Discover, A Time to Decide, Richard P. Olson, Valley Forge, PA: Judson Press, 1980.

Men in Mid-Life Crisis, Jim Conway, Elgin, IL: D.C. Cook, 1978.

Transition: The Stages of Adult Life, Charles M. Sell, Chicago: Moody Press, 1985.

From a secular perspective:

Transformations: Growth and Change in Adult Life, Robert Gould, New York: Simon and Schuster, 1978.

Season's of a Man's Life, Daniel J. Levinson, New York: Alfred A. Knopf, 1978.

Passages, Gail Sheehy, New York: Bantam, 1977.